Monetary Policy

Sujith Vijay

©2019 Sujith Vijay

All rights reserved.

ISBN-13: 978-1696321945

Cover image: *Bell Rock Lighthouse* by J.M.W. Turner

*Dedicated to the loving memory of my brother
Renjith Vijay (1985 - 2015)*

CONTENTS

- Chapter 1: Goals of Monetary Policy
- Chapter 2: Tools of Monetary Policy
- Chapter 3: Keynes and Friedman
- Story 1: The Weimar Republic
- Story 2: The 1937 Recession
- Story 3: Bretton Woods
- Story 4: The Triffin Testimony
- Story 5: The Nixon Shock
- Story 6: The 1973 Oil Crisis
- Story 7: The 1979 Oil Crisis
- Story 8: The Volcker Shock
- Story 9: The Lost Decade
- Story 10: The Greenspan Put
- Story 11: The Asian Financial Crisis
- Story 12: The Nasdaq Crash
- Story 13: Lehman Brothers
- Story 14: Quantitative Easing
- Chapter 4: The Impossible Trinity
- Chapter 5: Inflation Targeting
- Chapter 6: The Taylor Rule

Chapter 1: Goals of Monetary Policy

The origins of modern central banking can be traced to 17th century Europe with the advent of the *Riksen Ständers Bank* in 1668, run under the auspices of the Swedish parliament *Riksdag*. A couple of decades later, Charles Montagu, First Lord of the Treasury during the joint reign of King William III and Queen Mary II, drafted the Tonnage Act of 1694 that resulted in the formation of the Bank of England. The original purpose behind the formation of the bank was to raise 1.2 million pounds at 8% interest to finance the ongoing war against King Louis XIV of France. It was only in 1844 that the Bank of England was granted the exclusive right to issue currency notes against bullion reserves. The Riksen Ständers Bank changed its name to *Sveriges Riksbank* in 1866, and received a similar national monopoly on issuing currency in 1897. In the United States, the Federal Reserve system, consisting of twelve regional Federal Reserve banks, was created by an act of the United States Congress in 1913 during the presidency of Woodrow Wilson.

As macroeconomic theory evolved, the relationship between money supply and increases in prices was widely recognized. Central banks all over the world explored various ways to mitigate the effects of economic downturns and prolong the years of prosperity. Individual mistakes became collective lessons. A consensus soon emerged that the best path is one that kept inflation under control, as it was observed that large scale unemployment, foreclosures and bank failures often followed times when prices of essential goods and services spiralled out of control. Moreover, the effects of high inflation disproportionately affected the poor and widened economic inequality. Accordingly, **stable prices** became the primary mandate of central banks, and **maximum employment** became the secondary mandate. In practice, central banks also have a tertiary mandate – that of promoting **economic growth**. *Monetary policy* is an umbrella term used to describe the strategies used by a central bank to achieve these ends, in an environment of various economic headwinds and tailwinds.

Monetary policy works in tandem with *fiscal policy*, which is usually run by the Ministry of Finance or the Department of the Treasury, and concerns itself with taxation and government spending. Just as an independent judiciary is a prerequisite for a functional democracy, an independent monetary policy is a prerequisite for a functional economy. Modern democracies have acknowledged, sometimes grudgingly, the need for central bank independence, and modern central banks are invariably prepared for fallout from populist fiscal measures, especially ahead of elections. By and large, they live and let live.

There is arguably no other branch of human knowledge where the boundaries of perception and reality are as blurred as they are in economics. The universal law of gravitation will not decide to pull a prank on the third Friday of every other month just when Sir Isaac Newton was beginning to figure it all out. But in economics, and especially in financial markets, just when a good theory of individual and collective behaviour begins to explain observed phenomena and becomes common knowledge, the "smart money" adapts to the new theory and discrepancies start creeping in. It is a bit like quantum mechanics, where the mere act of measurement influences the magnitude of the measured quantity.

Monetary policy is said to be **expansionary** or accommodative when it aims to increase the money supply, and **contractionary** or restrictive when it does the opposite. The media often uses the adjectives *dovish* and *hawkish* to connote these two approaches. The art of central banking is to pivot from one of these approaches to the other as appropriate, or take a middle path, in a manner that inspires confidence and optimism (but preferably not euphoria) in citizens, corporations and capital markets. In the next chapter, we will explore the tools that central banks have at their disposal to achieve the aforementioned goals of monetary policy.

Chapter 2: Tools of Monetary Policy

How do central banks manage something as complicated as the collective money supply of an entire nation? The toolkit varies across nations, but the similarities vastly outnumber the differences. Central banks usually signal a change in monetary policy by altering the target for the benchmark interest rate, which in turn influences the cost of borrowing throughout the financial system. Thus a lower interest rate, all other things being equal (or as economists like to say, *ceteris paribus*), leads to easier credit conditions, greater velocity of money, and an expansion of the monetary base. Conversely, a higher interest rate leads to a tightening of credit and a contraction of the monetary base.

Lower interest rates tend to be conducive to economic growth, as the relatively lower interest burden boosts corporate profits and encourages new investment, wage increases and hiring. However, if credit conditions become too easy, it can lead to higher purchasing power in the short-term, thereby stoking inflation and eroding the value of the currency. Easy credit can also encourage speculation in risky assets like stocks and real estate, as the yield from safe havens like fixed deposits decreases due to the interest rate cut. Sooner or later, the asset bubble pops and the economy takes years to recover. According to the *Austrian Business Cycle Theory* pioneered by Ludwig von Mises and Friedrich Hayek, such boom and bust cycles are unavoidable in a world of fractional reserve banking, and central bank intervention often makes a bad situation worse. The Austrian School is by no means a fringe group of conspiracy theorists – Hayek was one of the early winners of the Nobel Memorial Prize in Economics, in 1974. Yet most mainstream economists do not take such a dim view of central banking, and believe that appropriate interventions ultimately have a beneficial effect on the economy.

When a central bank, or a committee of central bank members responsible for monetary policy, makes an announcement to the effect of lowering or raising interest rates, it is merely a signal of intent. The actual easing or tightening is usually accomplished by buying or selling government bonds in capital markets. Such activities are called **open market operations**, wherein the central bank indirectly influences the equilibrium interest rate by increasing or decreasing the supply of government bonds. Conceptually, this is analogous to the more familiar activities undertaken by a central bank to maintain the domestic currency at an appropriate exchange rate using its foreign currency reserves. In modern times, markets typically anticipate most of the actions of central banks ahead of time, so actual announcements of changes in interest rates are often not as disruptive as the unexpected economic events that lead to such changes in the first place.

A central bank is also *the lender of last resort* in an economy, and an effective tool for ensuring faster transmission of monetary policy to the banking sector is the **discount rate** – the interest rate at which the central bank makes short-term loans to commercial banks. The discount rate tends to be set somewhat higher than the target range for the benchmark interest rate, and the facility is typically availed only when the interbank lending limits have been breached. A change in the benchmark interest rate, like the Fed funds rate in the United States, is usually accompanied by a change in the discount rate as well. The difference is that the latter is set in stone with no real leeway, while the execution of the former is dependent on market forces, at least in principle. In practice, market forces are no match for a central bank that can print money at will, so all interest rates, including short-term deposits, long-term deposits, prime loans and subprime loans gravitate towards new equilibria associated with the changed benchmark interest rate.

A third channel for expanding or contracting the money supply is to modify the *reserve requirements* of banks. All banks are required to maintain the ratio of available cash to total reserves above a certain limit. Central banks can lower or raise this limit depending on whether they want to loosen or tighten credit conditions. For example, expansionary monetary policy is consistent with a lower reserve requirement, as banks are encouraged to lend more of their reserves, thereby increasing available credit by the *multiplier effect* of money. Lower reserve requirements tend to boost economic growth when times are good, but can lead to a cascade of bank failures when the economy goes south. When central banks are cautious and wish to contract the money supply, they tend to impose a higher reserve requirement.

All this is very well, you may say, but how do central banks decide whether to raise, lower or maintain benchmark interest rates? That, of course, is the trillion dollar question, and there are no easy answers. On 18 September 2019, a few days before the publication of this book, the Federal Reserve voted 7-3 to lower the Fed funds target range by 0.25%. The split decision should not be surprising, as central bank officials in charge of monetary policy are, to borrow a memorable phrase from Arthur Koestler, *"doing the work of prophets without their gift"*. They can only rely on their own judgement and the work of other scholars who have studied macroeconomic phenomena in the past. In the next chapter, we will encounter the work of two of the greatest minds in the history of modern economics, namely John Maynard Keynes and Milton Friedman, who have had a profound and lasting impact on the philosophy of modern central banking.

Chapter 3: Keynes and Friedman

All branches of natural and social sciences have evolved over a period of several centuries as intergenerational collaborative endeavours. Yet once in a while, a great visionary comes along and completely transforms the understanding of some academic discipline, often with the publication of a single book. Examples include Sir Isaac Newton's *Philosophiae Naturalis Principia Mathematica* in physics, Immanuel Kant's *Critique of Pure Reason* in philosophy and Sigmund Freud's *Interpretation of Dreams* in psychology. The natural candidate for such a position in economics is *The General Theory of Employment, Interest and Money* by John Maynard Keynes, published in 1936, a few years after the trough of the Great Depression.

The central argument of Keynes's book was that the finances of a nation should not be run like the finances of a household. In other words, while the appropriate response for a household facing hostile economic conditions is a reduction in spending, the appropriate response for a government under the same conditions is an increase in spending. Keynes postulated that increased government spending during recessions would help to boost aggregate demand in the economy, kindle *animal spirits* and ultimately lead to economic recovery. His essential insight was that the impact of expansionary policies, both fiscal and monetary, on inflation depended on the level of unemployment and economic growth. Keynes challenged the prevailing orthodoxy of the time, enshrined in the *quantity theory of money*, which posited that an increase in money supply always led to an increase in wages and prices. He conceded that increased government spending could lead to inflation in the long run, but as he observed in one of his earlier books, *"In the long run, we are all dead."*

So it is not as if economists had it all wrong before Keynes, but they had underestimated how long it took for prices to find a new equilibrium in response to an increase in money supply as predicted by their theory, especially during recessionary environments. Meanwhile, in the short term,

Keynes's remedies, which were mainly on the fiscal side, did wonders by bringing down unemployment and boosting economic growth. Central banks were able to implement monetary policy more effectively, with a judicious focus on all their mandates, rather than being overly worried about inflation all the time. The idea was that wages and prices were sticky during recessions – as long as there was residual slack in the economy, they would not rise much in response to greater demand, and sometimes would not rise at all. All this was put on a firm mathematical footing, partly by Keynes himself, and later by John Hicks and Alvin Hansen in their *IS-LM model*.

Keynes died in 1946, and by then his ideas had been widely accepted. In 1958, economist William Phillips built on Keynesian macroeconomic foundations and described an inverse relationship between inflation and unemployment. Under this model, the graph of inflation plotted as a function of unemployment traced a rectangular hyperbola, much like the graph of $y=1/x$, and this came to be known as the *Phillips Curve*. This academic development persuaded many central banks to pursue expansionist monetary policy in the hope that the costs of inflation would be mitigated by the benefits of lower unemployment.

Around the same time, the old quantity theory of money made a comeback in the United States in a new avatar called *Monetarism*. The principal exponent of Monetarism was Milton Friedman, a maverick economist at the University of Chicago. Friedman asserted that the reports of the assassination of the quantity theory of money by Keynes were greatly exaggerated, and succeeded in rehabilitating the essential tenets of the quantity theory by modifying the elasticity assumptions of the demand for money. He was also a vocal critic of the Phillips Curve, and maintained that a rapid increase in the money supply would result in high inflation without a corresponding decrease in unemployment. The stagflation episodes in the 1970s vindicated this view and enhanced Friedman's reputation. He also postulated a *natural rate of unemployment* below which the lack of mobility of jobs began to hurt the economy.

Friedman's influence extended beyond the University of Chicago, where he was a faculty member. Economics departments in the United States aligned towards two rival camps – the *freshwater school* consisting of campuses close to the Great Lakes, and the *saltwater school* consisting of campuses on the West Coast and the East Coast. The former group, including the University of Chicago, Carnegie Mellon University, Cornell University and the University of Rochester, had great faith in the power of the free market to fix malaises in the economy, just as Friedman did. The latter group, including Harvard University, Princeton University, Yale University and the University of California, Berkeley, advocated periodic governmental intervention to rebalance aggregate demand, just as Keynes did. Modern macroeconomics has been shaped in large measure by contributions from both these schools.

Story 1: The Weimar Republic

After four years of unprecedented bloodshed and destruction, the First World War came to an end on 11 November 1918 following the truce between the Allied Powers and Germany. The initial truce was only for 36 days, but it was extended several times, culminating in the Treaty of Versailles in 1919. Among the conditions in the treaty were astronomical sums of money to be paid by Germany as reparations for war to the victorious nations. Over the years, this put an enormous strain on the fiscal position of the Weimar republic, the postwar German government named after the city where the new constituent assembly first met.

By 1923, Germany began to default on the reparation payments. In retaliation, the French and Belgian troops took over the Ruhr valley, an area rich in coal and other natural resources. This put further strain on the German economy, and *Reichsbank* (the German central bank) responded by printing paper money as a last-ditch effort to control debt. The German government had already abandoned its currency peg to gold shortly after the commencement of the First World War. The Goldmark, whose value was pegged to gold by the equation *1 kg gold = 2790 Goldmark* was replaced by the paper currency known as *Papiermark*. The paper currency was backed by German reputation and pretty much nothing else. Reputation being a fickle animal, the Papiermark, which began at par with the erstwhile Goldmark, started eroding rapidly after Germany's loss in the war. The exchange rate between the US dollar and the Papiermark rose from 4.2 (i.e, 4.2 Papiermark= 1 US dollar) in August 1914 to 320 in June 1922, and further to 7400 in December 1922. Yet this was just the beginning of the storm.

As we noted earlier, the Reichsbank started printing money in an attempt to purchase enough hard currency (e.g. the US dollar and the British pound) to meet its expenses, including reparations. This eroded the value of the currency and forced the bank to print even more paper money. The expectation of currency depreciation among the general public became a self-fulfilling prophecy. The exchange rate of the Papiermark with the US Dollar skyrocketed from 7400 in December 1922 to *one million* in June 1923 and **4.2 trillion** in November 1923. Pretty much the same rate as August 1914, except for that annoying bit about the trillion. So a new currency called Rentenmark, with twelve fewer zeroes (i.e., 1 Rentenmark = 1 trillion Papiermark) was launched on 16 November 1923. Four days later, Rudolf Havenstein, the Reichsbank president under whose watch the hyperinflation drama played out, died of a heart attack.

Meanwhile, the unemployment rate had increased from 2.8% in December 1922 to 23.4% in November 1923. Seven articles of the Weimar constitution had been suspended in September 1923 and the nation was under emergency provisions. General Erich Ludendorff and a young politician named Adolf Hitler had just attempted an unsuccessful coup d'etat known as the *Beer Hall Putsch*. The new Reichsbank president, Hjalmar Schacht, had his work cut out for him. He knew that getting out of the mess they found themselves in would take a lot more than erasing a few zeroes from the currency.

The new Rentenmark, unlike the old Goldmark, was not convertible to gold. Instead, its value was tied to the capital reserves of Reichsbank, which included a "forced mortgage" of 4% of all the private agricultural land and industrial property in Germany. These "real estate bonds" yielded its owners 6% annual interest, and these interest payments were indexed to gold. Additionally, the Reichsbank would no longer fund government spending through the new currency. The initial money supply was limited to 500 million Rentenmarks.

Currency speculators continued to raid the Rentenmark as they did with the Papiermark. However, interest payments on borrowed money, now indexed to foreign currencies like the dollar and the pound, were no longer favourable for indiscriminate short selling. By now, the *Franc* had depreciated as well, and speculators took the train to the safer pastures of Paris. The reparation terms under the Treaty of Versailles were revised in 1924 to a staggered payment plan under the mediation of Charles Dawes, who won the Nobel Peace Prize in 1925 for his efforts. Unemployment peaked at 30%, and real interest rates remained quite high for a long time, but the nightmare ended by late 1924.

As we now know, the real nightmare was only beginning. The erosion of wealth would provide fertile ground for the emergence of the Nazi ideology and the eventual election of Adolf Hitler in 1933. The British journalist and author Adam Fergusson, in his book *When Money Dies*, describes the recovery and repercussions as follows:

> Sanity had returned to Germany's finances; and no doubt 1924, a period of often extreme monetary stringency, consolidated the financial recovery. But it was too much to hope after the Dawes Plan was adopted in August and unemployment dwindled encouragingly throughout the summer and autumn, that years of reckless profligacy could be so easily paid for,

or what the country had passed through would have no lasting effects on the people's minds. The destitution of the middle classes, of whom the resilient would recover in due course, was only part of the price. The economic reckoning was still to come. Some would say that the political reckoning did not come until 1933, when economic recovery had to begin again.

Story 2: The 1937 Recession

"Stock prices have reached what looks like a permanently high plateau," proclaimed Yale economist Irving Fisher on 16 October 1929. Seven days later, the stock market crashed, marking the beginning of the Great Depression. The Dow Jones Index, after rising steadily from 63.90 in August 1921 to 381.17 in September 1929, dropped below 200 by mid-November, and would bottom out at 41.22 in July 1932. The share price of Radio Corporation of America, after pole vaulting from $11 in 1924 to $114 in 1929, fell below $3 in 1932. It would only be in 1954 that the Dow would reclaim the peak levels seen in 1929.

The carnage did not stop with speculators and investors. Nor was it confined to the United States. Global GDP is estimated to have declined by 15% between 1929 and 1932. Unemployment peaked at 25% in the United States, 27% in Canada, 29% in Australia and 30% in Germany. Industrial production declined 47% in the United States, 42% in Canada, 31% in France and 16% in Britain. The prices of coffee, cotton and rubber fell from the September 1929 levels by nearly 50% in just fifteen months. Among the US policies that are blamed for aggravating the slump was the *Smoot-Hawley Tariff Act of 1930*, which led to retaliatory tariffs by Canada and France, and an increase in income tax in 1932.

The tide began to turn when the 1932 re-election bid of President Herbert Hoover was thwarted by a charismatic visionary named Franklin D. Roosevelt. He unleashed a series of federal recovery projects and reforms under the umbrella term *New Deal*. The US dollar was devalued by making it illegal to own bullion in 1933 and altering the exchange rate between gold and the dollar from 20.67 dollars per (troy) ounce to 35 dollars per ounce in 1934. The weaker dollar allowed an expansionist monetary policy. By 1936, unemployment had decreased to 17% and the GDP had recovered most of the lost ground from 1929. What we now call the Great Depression was looking more like a prolonged recession back then.

And then the Federal Reserve blundered. Driven by a fear of inflation, the money supply was tightened by doubling the reserve requirements for banks in 1936. This had the effect of withdrawing the monetary stimulus that had spearheaded the gradual economic recovery. The mandates of price stability and balanced economic growth had come into conflict, and the Fed guessed wrong.

The impact was immediate. Unemployment jumped from 14% in 1937 to 19% in 1938. The GDP flipped from an annual growth of 5.1% in 1937 to a decline of 3.3% in 1938. Deflation reared its ugly head for the first time since 1932. A full recovery from this second downturn would have to wait until the next decade, when the US involvement in the Second World War led to a large increase in aggregate demand and a sharp drop in unemployment.

It certainly did not help that the United States Treasury, in December 1936, launched a gold sterilization programme that would prevent gold inflows from becoming part of the monetary base. Milton Friedman and Anna Schwartz, in their book *A Monetary History of the United States, 1867-1960* describe the consequences of these policies as follows:

> *The combined impact of the rise in reserve requirements and – no less important – the Treasury gold sterilization program first sharply reduced the rate of increase in the monetary stock and then converted it into a decline. From June 1936 to June 1937, the money stock grew at the continuous annual rate of 4.2% per year and then in the following year fell at the rate of 2.4%.*

In a conference held in 2002 on the occasion of the 90th birthday of Milton Friedman, Federal Reserve governor and future Fed Chair Ben Bernanke acknowledged the above criticism with the following words:

> "Let me end my talk by abusing slightly my status as an official representative of the Federal Reserve. I would like to say to Milton and Anna: Regarding the Great Depression, you're right. We did it. We're very sorry. But thanks to you, we won't do it again."

Anyone who has watched the actions of the Federal Reserve since September 2008 would agree that they have indicated *zero interest* in doing it again!

Story 3: Bretton Woods

In July 1944, at the height of the madness described by Kurt Vonnegut as *"Western Civilization's second unsuccessful attempt to commit suicide"*, 730 delegates from 44 nations assembled at the Mount Washington Hotel in Bretton Woods, New Hampshire for the *United Nations Monetary Conference.* At the conclusion of the conference, the delegates signed the Bretton Woods Agreement, agreeing to establish the *International Bank for Reconstruction and Development* (IBRD), which would become the principal arm of the World Bank group of institutions, as well as the *International Monetary Fund* (IMF). The goal of these institutions would be to foster a spirit of economic cooperation and coordination between nations rather than competition and rivalry. Particular emphasis was given to maintaining stable exchange rates between national currencies and curbing excessive speculation in the foreign exchange market. There was widespread agreement that international coordination was required to keep various currencies at optimal strengths so that accommodative policies and a worldwide monetary expansion, as was necessary during the Great Depression, could continue without creating capital and commodity imbalances across borders.

It was no coincidence that such a meeting happened in the middle of a worldwide war. Cordell Hull, the US Secretary of State and principal architect of the United Nations Charter, saw both World Wars as fundamentally rooted in economic causes. He reasoned that international coordination in trade and monetary policy was an important prerequisite in avoiding such internecine conflicts going forward. Although Hull did not attend the Bretton Woods conference, his vision of a world largely devoid of trade barriers was broadly implemented due to the negotiating skills of Harry Dexter White, who headed the US delegation. White's legacy would later be severely tarnished due to credible allegations of Soviet espionage, but it is generally agreed that in 1944, he was acting in the best interest of global economic stability. If he had a conflict of interest at all, it was in ensuring that the US dollar would be the reserve currency of the world.

White did not have an easy task, as many of his ideas ran into disagreements from the British delegation led by John Maynard Keynes himself. History has vindicated many of the objections raised by Keynes, but the real takeaway from Bretton Woods was the worldwide recognition of a sea change in the balance of global power. Benn Steil, in his comprehensive book *The Battle for Bretton Woods* describes the proposals of Keynes as follows:

The basic mechanics of what became known as the Keynes Plan were more complex, and certainly more ambitious than those of the White Plan. International transactions would be settled through a new International Clearing Union (ICU). Neither the national central banks nor the ICU would actually hold foreign currency. The national central banks would buy and sell their own currencies among themselves by means of credits and debits, denominated in newly created bank money to the clearing accounts of the ICU. Keynes would later call this bank money bancor (literally 'bank gold' in French). Bancor was to have a fixed exchange rate with all members' currencies and gold. In addition to acquiring bancor through trade, national and central banks could add bancor credits to their clearing account by paying in gold. But they would not be allowed to redeem bancor for gold; bancor could only be used for transfers into other national central bank clearing accounts. This unusual asymmetry was a reflection of Keynes's central idea that the ICU should be a tool for encouraging the growth of money in circulation globally, and for putting up barriers against monetary contraction.

These ideas were far ahead of their time, and were considerably diluted by the American delegation, who had overwhelming economic and political clout at the time. What emerged in the end was not a clearing union, but the International Monetary Fund. While there was no global currency like *bancor*, all member nations agreed to maintain their exchange rates within 1% by pegging their currencies to gold, except in the event of a fundamental disequilibrium. In practice, the US dollar was pegged at 35 dollars per ounce of gold, while other currencies were pegged to the dollar. The US government guaranteed the full convertibility of foreign dollar reserves for gold. This made the US dollar the *de facto* reserve currency of the world. The International Monetary Fund would provide liquidity to bridge temporary deficits in the balance of payment. The upshot was that no country could engage in competitive devaluation to obtain an advantage in international trade. The IMF was formally launched in 1947, a year after the launch of the International Bank for Reconstruction and Development (IBRD), the other major achievement of the Bretton Woods Conference.

Story 4: The Triffin Testimony

As we have seen, the Bretton Woods conference firmly established the US dollar as the reserve currency of the world. The guarantee of full convertibility of dollars to gold incentivized many foreign governments to accumulate US dollars. By the late 1950s, it was clear that there will soon be more US dollars in global circulation than gold reserves in the vaults of the United States Treasury.

In 1960, Robert Triffin, a Belgian-American economist and professor at Yale University, testified before the US Congress that the Bretton Woods system had severe structural flaws and was unsustainable in the long run. The system had worked very well in the aftermath of the war when the United States had a budget surplus. But the massive reconstruction program of Europe with American aid known as the *Marshall Plan*, coupled with a large increase in defence spending, soon turned the surplus into a deficit. Eventually, a high deficit would erode faith in the US dollar, forcing the US government to curtail the availability of dollars overseas, leading to a global recession. Triffin argued that any nation issuing a global reserve currency would eventually have to choose between the interests of its own citizens and the interests of citizens of other nations whose demand was responsible for the reserve currency status in the first place.

The following excerpt from Triffin's statement before the US Congress outlined the gravity of the situation and the need to act quickly:

"A fundamental reform of the international monetary system has long been overdue. Its necessity and urgency are further highlighted today by the imminent threat to the once mighty US dollar. Both problems are closely intertwined and should be attached together.

I have abundantly discussed elsewhere the reforms of the International Monetary Fund that would seem best suited both to help us solve right now the dollar crisis, and to forestall, later on, a world liquidity crisis. As usual, however, administrative complacency and inertia have continued so far to oppose apparently insurmountable obstacles to the simple and obvious remedies at hand."

Triffin's essential argument was that the US dollar could not have two disparate functions at the same time, namely the currency of the United States and the dominant global reserve currency. Keynes had anticipated this difficulty during the Bretton Woods conference, and had proposed the *bancor* precisely for these reasons. At the time, his objections were overruled as the US delegation never anticipated that their country would pivot so soon from a trade surplus to a trade deficit. But even after the truth was staring them in the face, politicians and bureaucrats continued to ignore the wisdom of economists like Keynes and Triffin, as they so often do. They just kicked the can down the road until the road itself came to a dead end.

Story 5: The Nixon Shock

The Bretton Woods system died suddenly and unexpectedly in the middle of a televised speech by US President Richard Nixon on Sunday, 15 August 1971, when the President announced his decision to unilaterally abandon the convertibility of US dollars to gold. There were several factors that led to this decision. The London Gold Pool, a consortium of central banks that had pooled their gold reserves since 1961 in an effort to maintain the fixed exchange rate between the US dollar and gold, collapsed in March 1968. Shortly thereafter, the US Congress repealed the 25% gold backing that was mandatory for fresh dollar issuance, ushering in the fiat currency era. West Germany left the Bretton Woods system in May 1971. In the next three months, the *Deutsche Mark* appreciated 7.5% against the US dollar. On 9th August, Switzerland also abandoned the Bretton Woods agreement. Yet the IMF and Nixon's own State Department were not told about the President's decision, and were taken by surprise on 15th August.

Nixon packaged his decision quite well, and there was initially a chorus of domestic approval, including from mainstream newspapers like *The New York Times*. Nixon had also announced a temporary surcharge of 10% on imports to ensure that the expected turbulence in foreign exchange rates did not adversely affect American products. The Dow Jones Index rose 3.8% the day after the announcement. The following excerpt from his address was characteristic of the old trick of marketing an act of desperation as sublime strategy:

> "Let me lay to rest the bugaboo of what is called devaluation. If you want to buy a foreign car or take a trip abroad, market conditions may cause your dollar to buy slightly less. But if you are among the overwhelming majority of Americans who buy American-made products in America, your dollar will be worth just as much tomorrow as it is today. The effect of this action, in other words, will be to stabilize the dollar.
>
> Now, this action will not win us any friends among the international money traders. But our

primary concern is with the American workers, and with fair competition around the world."

After months of negotiations, a new set of exchange rates with a considerably devalued dollar were agreed upon in December 1971 at a meeting of the ten most influential member nations of the IMF. The dollar was now pegged at 38 dollars per ounce of gold, with the margin of fluctuations set at 2.25%. This was known as the *Smithsonian Agreement*, and Nixon had hailed it as a new chapter in international economics. Yet the arrangement was short-lived. After a second devaluation to 42 dollars per ounce of gold, the United States gave up entirely on fixed exchange rates in March 1973 and allowed the dollar to float in the open market.

The dollar had already been a fiat currency in the aftermath of the 1968 collapse of the London Gold Pool, but now it was a *floating* fiat currency that had to find its fair price against gold. And it seemed in no hurry to do that. By September 1973, the Federal Reserve had raised the funds rate to 11% from

5% in November 1971. This was necessitated by a rapid spike in inflation from 3.3% to 7.4% during the same period.

It could be argued that the 1971 interest rates were artificially low to begin with, and that Fed Chair Arthur Burns had bowed to political pressure from Nixon to avoid an economic slowdown ahead of his re-election. After all, another desperate measure that Nixon took to ensure his re-election would eventually lead to his resignation in 1974. The only silver lining was the low unemployment numbers, in accordance with Keynesian theory and the Phillips curve. But that too would change in the coming years, as a new spectre was about to haunt America – the spectre of stagflation.

Story 6: The 1973 Oil Crisis

On 6 October 1973, Jewish people all over the world, especially those in Israel, were observing *Yom Kippur* (The Day of Atonement), the holiest day of Judaism. Decreed as a strict day of rest in the Torah, the Yom Kippur Day of 1973 was chosen by a coalition of Arab states led by Egypt and Syria to mount a surprise two-pronged attack on Israel, simultaneously from the Sinai Peninsula and the Golan Heights. Although Israeli Prime Minister Golda Meir and defence minister Moshe Dayan had credible intelligence reports about an impending attack, they strategically decided against a pre-emptive strike in order to maximize the chances of American support. The ensuing hostilities lasted nearly three weeks, and Israel's eventual victory, with considerable aid from the United States, was far from the comprehensive rout that it had inflicted on the combined forces of Egypt, Syria, Jordan and Iraq in the Six-Day War of 1967.

During the course of the war, several Arab members of the Organization of Petroleum

Exporting Countries (OPEC), in solidarity with the belligerents, raised oil prices by 70% and announced the first of a series of production cuts. Additionally, an embargo was imposed on the Allies of Israel, including the United States, the Netherlands, South Africa and Portugal. For several months after the end of the war, the production cuts escalated until the price of crude oil (West Texas Intermediate) per barrel climbed from $4.31 in October 1973 to $10.11 in January 1974. On 12 February 1974, the US Secretary of State Henry Kissinger unveiled *Project Independence* with the explicit objective of making the United States energy independent. The embargo ended a month later, after a joint statement by Arab oil ministers, without achieving the stated goal of forcing Israel to withdraw to pre-1967 borders.

The oil embargo had a severe and devastating effect on the economies of nearly all industrialized nations. The United States GDP contracted during four of the five quarters between January 1974 and March 1975. The Dow Jones Index fell by 43% between September 1973 and November 1974.

Unemployment increased from 4.8% in September 1973 to 9.0% in May 1975. In a development that took economists by surprise, the high unemployment rate was accompanied by high inflation, which stayed stubbornly above 9% throughout 1974 and the first half of 1975. According to Keynesian economics and the Phillips curve, the two could not coexist at the same time, and yet there they were. The term *stagflation,* originally coined in 1965 by British politician Iain Macleod to describe a similar, if somewhat milder, situation in the United Kingdom, was widely used to describe the mess.

It may be worthwhile to revisit the reasons for the implicit faith economists had in the Phillips curve in the first place. The Great Depression had a profound impact on the priorities of macroeconomics, and inflation was considered a benign side effect of the economic growth necessary to ensure full employment. Moreover, any rise in unemployment was expected to automatically reduce inflation due to the decrease in consumer spending and aggregate demand. Inflation was still a concern for economists, but only when unemployment was at very low levels, say around the so-called *natural rate* of 4%. A Keynesian economist watching the figures of 9% inflation and 9% unemployment in 1975 might as well have been an open-mouthed eight-year-old watching King Kong climb the Empire State Building. Milton Friedman and the Monetarist school ripped the Phillips curve apart, and the resulting policy chaos eventually led to the rise of a new brand of economics and politics, championed by Ronald Reagan in the United States and Margaret Thatcher in the United Kingdom.

The profound lesson the stagflation episode gave economists was that inflationary expectations were as important as inflation itself. (This idea would soon be put on a sound theoretical footing by economists like Charles Goodhart, Robert Lucas Jr., Thomas Sargent and Neil Wallace, under the rubric of *rational expectations*.) The Fed funds rate changed quite erratically between 1972 and 1975, climbing from 3.25% in February 1972 to 11% in September 1973, dropping to 9% in February 1974, rising again and peaking at 13% in July

1974 before plunging to 5.25% in May 1975. None of this inspired any confidence in markets or the economy, and corporations believed, quite correctly, that the Federal Reserve had lost control of anchoring inflation expectations. Prices never came down because businesses did not feel comfortable lowering them, as nobody knew what the Fed would do next. Hiring never picked up as there was a gap between what prospective employees expected due to inflation, and what businesses could afford due to the recession. The faith of American citizens in government was also at an all-time low, due to the Watergate Scandal and betrayal in high places. In short, the stagflation was as much due to a credibility crisis as it was due to the supply shock of high oil prices.

    The same sad opera played on the other side of the Atlantic, with the United Kingdom eventually requiring an IMF bailout. Inflation figures were far worse than those in the United States, peaking at 26% in August 1976. GDP growth was negative during five of the eight quarters between October 1973 and September 1975. However, the unemployment figures were not too bad, at 5.8%. Indeed, the precise connotation of the term *stagflation* varies among economists. High inflation is always implied, but whether it is accompanied by economic contraction or high unemployment, depends on the context. Usually there is no confusion, as they are as chummy as Laurel and Hardy.

High inflation led to rapid depreciation of the British pound and ultimately a balance of payment crisis. The IMF had to step in with a loan of $3.9 billion, in return for austerity measures and a clear plan to reduce the fiscal deficit. Prime Minister James Callaghan, speaking at the Labour Party conference, was forced to concede that the Keynesian paradigm was not a panacea for all economic ills:

"We used to think that you could spend your way out of a recession and increase employment by cutting taxes and boosting government spending. I tell you in all candour that that option no longer exists, and in so far as it ever did exist, it only worked on each occasion since the war by injecting a bigger dose of

inflation into the economy, followed by a higher level of unemployment as the next step."

Story 7: The 1979 Oil Crisis

On 16 January 1979, Mohammad Reza Pahlavi, the Shah of Iran, fled to Egypt, abdicating his throne and putting his Prime Minister Shapour Bakhtiyar in charge. There was widespread discontent in the country during the final years of the Shah's rule, and the Iranian oil industry had ground to a halt by December 1978 as part of the nationwide strikes and protests. By April 1979, the Iranian regime changed from a pro-Western monarchy to an Islamic theocracy. Yet Ayatollah Khomeini, who had led the revolution from exile and had become the head of the new government, did not immediately succeed in restoring oil exports to prior levels.

Unlike 1973, the oil supply in international markets had not contracted significantly, as Saudi Arabia picked up most of the slack caused by the drop in Iranian exports. Yet memories of the earlier oil crisis were raw, and the US government had to impose rationing to stem the panic buying of motorists. The price of WTI crude oil per barrel jumped from $14.85 in December 1978 to $39.50 in April 1980. The political situation was aggravated by a hostage crisis in the US embassy in Tehran that began in November 1979 and was resolved only in January 1981.

The rapid rise in oil prices brought back double-digit inflation. The US dollar weakened dramatically during the tenure of Fed Chair William Miller. The exchange rate for the British pound against the US dollar climbed from 1.91 in March 1978, when Miller took office to 2.24 in August 1979, when he was replaced by Paul Volcker. The price of gold per ounce rose from $190 to $283 during the same period, marking the beginning of a bubble in precious metals, with gold eventually topping out at $850 per ounce and silver at $49 per ounce in early 1980. These levels would not be seen again until 2007 and 2011, respectively.

Miller had increased the Fed funds rate from 6.75% to 10.6% during his seventeen months in office, but history has not been kind to him. It is widely believed that his actions were not enough, as the Federal Reserve ended up merely playing catchup with inflation, which rose from 6.6% to 11.8% during the same period. In other words, Miller pursued a reactive policy when the circumstances demanded proactive action.

Miller did succeed in staving off a recession, and that was his stated reason for not pursuing more aggressive monetary policy. Yet his policies are considered to have aggravated the fallout from the Iranian oil crisis. It might seem unfair to blame the Fed for contractionary monetary policy in 1937 and also for relatively accommodative policy in 1978, but the situations were drastically different. The annual inflation in 1937 was only 2.9%, and the GDP growth, though healthy, was at a four-year-low. The annual inflation in 1978 was 9.0% and the GDP growth was at a five-year-high. Modern consensus, except among economists on the far left of the political spectrum, appears to be that the Fed should have raised rates decisively to break the back of inflation once and for all, even if it meant a couple of quarters of mild contraction. That is exactly what Miller's successor Paul Volcker did, leading to decades of prosperity and the US economy as we know it now.

Story 8: The Volcker Shock

On 6 October 1979, Pope John Paul II visited President Jimmy Carter at his residence, marking the first ever papal visit to the White House. In the next day's newspapers, however, this historic visit was scooped in importance by an emergency press conference held by Fed Chair Paul Volcker the same evening. Volcker announced that the Federal Reserve had an emergency meeting earlier in the day and had decided on a shift in the implementation of monetary policy, changing the focus from a targeted Fed funds rate to managing the volume of banking reserves. With inflation already running at 12.1%, such a move raised many eyebrows, as it was guaranteed to bring turbulence to capital markets as well as the economy. Volcker had done to the funds rate what Nixon had done to the dollar.

What was the Fed thinking? Here is what Volcker told a reporter who had essentially asked him that question, albeit politely:

"The Federal Reserve for some years has ordered a good deal of its emphasis in actual day-

to-day operations, to maintaining a high degree of stability in the Federal funds rate which we most directly influence. That rate, of course, has been influenced in one direction, but generally by small increments in order to effect the growth in the money supply. Now what is implied here is a somewhat different approach – where the primary emphasis is put on the supply of reserves which ultimately controls the money supply. I don't want to suggest that the control is so precise that it works week by week or even with precision month by month. But by emphasizing the supply of reserves and constraining the growth of the money supply through the reserve mechanism, we think we can get firmer control over the growth in the money supply in a shorter period of time – greater assurance of that result. But the other side of the coin is, in supplying the reserves in that manner, the daily rate in the market – the rate without in itself of great economic significance – is apt to fluctuate over a wider range than has been the practice in recent years."

"Fluctuate over a wider range" turned out to be an understatement. By March 1980, the Fed funds rate had reached 17.2%, and inflation finally topped out at 14.8%. But that can only be known in hindsight, and the Fed continued tightening for one more month. After April 1980, the funds rate fell off a cliff, and by July, it had dropped from 17.6% to 9%. Then the tightening started again, until the rate reached 19% in January 1981, fell to 14.7% in March, reached 19% again in June, before finally starting its long downward slide to 12.4% in December, and 9.5% by October 1982. Meanwhile, the annoyingly persistent inflation finally dipped below 8.0% in February 1982 for the first time in 42 months, and had dropped to 4.6% by October 1982. At this point, the Federal Reserve returned to its old approach of targeting the Fed funds rate.

All this firefighting came at enormous cost to the public – particularly farmers, homebuilders, manufacturing workers and the American middle class. The price to pay was not one recession, but two. The automobile industry, to name one sector of the economy, was furious at Volcker. Lee Iacocca recalls in his autobiography how the fluctuating Fed funds rate impacted the precarious recovery of Chrysler:

By December we had run into another problem. The prime rate had now zoomed up to 18.5 percent. Two months earlier, when the K-cars were first introduced, interest rates had been 5 percent lower. If they had stayed at 13.5 percent, we could have sold a lot of cars. But in those days, interest rates were changing almost daily. And cars as well as houses were going unsold.

I was furious with the Fed's mercurial behavior on interest rates, but there was nothing I could do to change it. I could, however, respond to the situation. And I did.

To fight the specter of high interest rates, we came up with a floating rebate plan. We would grant a refund to any customer who bought a car on credit – based on the difference between 13 percent and the prevailing interest rate when the car was purchased.

When I announced the new plan, I said: "The Lord helps those who help themselves." He must have been listening, although Paul Volcker was not, because our gamble paid off. Before long, Ford and GM were offering rebates of their own.

Businesses had to improvise like that, or they would go bankrupt. Nobody knew what was coming next, not even Volcker. In 1980, the economy contracted by 8.0% in the second quarter, contracted by another 0.5% in the third quarter, and expanded by 7.7% in the fourth quarter. Going by the technical definition of a recession as two consecutive quarters of economic contraction, there was a recession in 1980. But it was over before you knew it, and the unemployment rate never crossed 8%. However, inflation stayed above 12% throughout 1980, necessitating more aggressive monetary policy during the first half of 1981.

From October 1981 to September 1982, inflation declined steadily from 10.1% to 5.0%. That was the good news. Everything else was bad news. GDP contracted in three of the four quarters during that period. Unemployment climbed from 7.9% all the way to 10.1%. The second recession was serious. Keynesians were grinning to the extent it was socially acceptable under the circumstances. The Phillips curve had returned.

And then the tide turned. The economic contraction during the third quarter of 1982 would be followed by not one, not two, but *thirty-two* consecutive quarters of economic expansion. Unemployment would peak at 10.8% in December 1982, dip below 8% in February 1984, and would not rise above 8% again for *twenty-five years*. Inflation, which had dipped below 7% in July 1982, has not risen above 7% *ever again*. Good times were back, at least in the United States.

Story 9: The Lost Decade

It should come as no surprise that the Dow Jones Index, the London FTSE, the German DAX, the South Korean Kospi, the Indian Sensex, and indeed nearly all national benchmark stock indices, are trading in 2019 at or near lifetime highs. However, there is one major stock market that set its lifetime high way back in 1989, and has not reached 70% of that level even *once* since 1991. We are talking about Japan, a nation that was widely expected to overtake the United States as the world's largest economy by the mid-1990s. In 1989, the five biggest companies in the world by market capitalization were all Japanese. Since then, the Japanese economy has had to grapple for nearly fifteen years with a painfully long recession and a nightmarish deflationary spiral that has had a profound impact on the psyche of the nation.

For the ten-year period between 1992 and 2002, dubbed *The Lost Decade*, the Japanese GDP was essentially unchanged. Moreover, this was not just the real GDP – even the nominal GDP was flat. The annualized nominal GDP growth rate and inflation rate for the 1992-2002 period were 0.52% and 0.16%, were respectively. Since there was practically no inflation, there was no need to adjust anything for inflation.

Such disasters usually do not happen due to a single mistake, and the seeds of the malaise were sown during the mid-1980s, which was a time of easy credit and excessive accommodation. When the asset bubble in stocks and real estate finally popped between 1989 and 1991, it led to a cascade of bank failures and business closures. The Basel I Capital Accord of 1988, which called for a minimum capital reserve ratio of 8% to be implemented by G-10 nations by the end of 1992, also contributed to the credit crunch.

The Lost Decade, like the Great Depression, was fundamentally a balance sheet crisis. The precipitous drop in aggregate demand was a result of everyone trying to reduce debt at the same time. Economist Richard Koo, in his book *The Holy Grail of Macroeconomics,* illustrates this quandary:

When a nationwide plunge in asset prices eviscerates asset values, leaving only the debt behind, the private sector begins paying down debt en masse. As a result, the broader economy experiences something economists call a "fallacy of composition". This occurs when behavior that would be right for one person (or company) leads to an undesirable outcome when engaged in by all people (or companies). Japan's economy has suffered from this fallacy often over the last fifteen years.

Mistakes were made during the recovery as well. Kiichi Miyazawa, the Prime Minister from November 1991 to August 1993, tried the textbook solutions of Keynesian firefighting by ramping up government expenditure. However, most of the necessary infrastructure spending had already been done in a developed economy like Japan, so the government ended up building roads and bridges to nowhere – most of it was money down the drain. Miyazawa's Liberal Democratic Party was voted out of power in the next elections, for the first time in 38 years. Unstable coalition governments ruled Japan for the next three years, and soon the LDP was back in power. The damage was complete when Ryutaro Hashimoto, the Prime Minister from January 1996 to July 1998, nipped a potential recovery in the bud by raising the value-added consumption tax from 3% to 5%.

Monetary policy wasn't particularly inspired either. Overspeeding during good times was followed by oversteering during bad times. The rate of growth of the monetary base fluctuated widely, from 6% in 1987 to 12% in 1989, plunging to 2% in 1992, back to 6% in 1994, down to 4% in 1995, and zooming to 10% in 1996. Compounding the woes of deflation was the steady appreciation of the Japanese yen, rising from an exchange rate of 158 versus the dollar in April 1990 to 83 in April 1995. Economist John Makin, in his comprehensive paper *Japan's Lost Decade: Lessons for America* summarizes the policy mistakes made by the Bank of Japan as follows:

While the Bank of Japan's insensitivity to gyrations in the growth rate of the monetary base may seem hard to explain, the reason lies clearly in its tendency to focus on the level of interest rates as a guide to monetary policy. The danger of doing this in an environment of disinflation, deflation, and weak investment spending was clearly articulated in the Friedman-Schwartz Monetary History, which focused on the U.S. experience during the 1930s. Market interest rates reflect underlying real returns on investment and market inflationary expectations. After an equity market collapse accompanied by sharply lower investment spending, real interest rates drop, signaling economic weakness, not easier monetary policy. As an economy slows and prices fall, lower inflationary expectations also contribute to lower market interest rates. This too signals more economic weakness than it does ease of monetary policy.

Towards the end of the Lost Decade, the Bank of Japan made one major policy innovation, known as *quantitative easing*. With interest rates already near zero, they embarked on a huge expansion of their balance sheet in March 2001 by announcing *open-ended* purchases of long-term government bonds and commercial paper, as opposed to intermittent purchases intended to coax interest rates to the desired level as is done during open market operations. This led to a flood of liquidity and alleviated the credit crunch prevailing in the markets. Additionally, the Bank of Japan committed to maintain the overnight lending rate at zero as long as deflation persisted in the economy. This led to moderate economic stimulation, and the deflationary era was essentially over by late 2003. Yet this innovation was dismissed by economists as a desperate remedy for desperate times and essentially a one-off event. Little did they know that in just a few years, every central bank in the developed world would be emulating the Bank of Japan and pursuing their own versions of quantitative easing.

Story 10: The Greenspan Put

Perhaps the lasting legacy of self-styled philosopher and strident haranguer Ayn Rand will not be the Objectivist movement she founded or her sharply polarizing books like *Fountainhead* and *Atlas Shrugged*. She is likely to be remembered for the tremendous influence she had on the economic philosophy of Alan Greenspan, chairman of the Federal Reserve from 1987 to 2006. A member of Rand's inner circle in the 1960s and contributor to the Objectivist Newsletter, Greenspan was the most powerful voice in global finance for nearly two decades. Markets listened with bated breath to his pronouncements and prognostications. The opening paragraph of Robert Shiller's classic book *Irrational Exuberance* describes a well-known example as follows:

When Alan Greenspan, as chairman of the Federal Reserve Board, first used the term irrational exuberance to describe the behavior of stock market investors, the world fixated on those words. He spoke at a black-tie dinner in Washington, D.C., on December 5, 1996, and the televised speech was followed the world over. As soon as he uttered these words, stock markets dropped precipitously. In Japan, the Nikkei index dropped 3.2%; in Hong Kong, the Hang Seng dropped 2.9%; and in Germany, the DAX dropped 4%. In London, the FTSE100 was down 4% at one point during the day, and in the United States, the next morning, the Dow Jones Industrial Average was down 2.3% near the beginning of trading. The sharp reaction of the markets all over the world to those two words in the middle of a staid and unremarkable speech seemed absurd. This event made for an amusing story about the craziness of markets, a story that was told for a time around the world.

Greenspan didn't earn this influence overnight. Two months into his tenure as Fed Chair, he helped stem the damage from the *Black Monday* crash of 19 October 1987, when the Dow Jones Index dropped 22.6% in a single day, breaking the record set during the Great Depression era. Greenspan issued a one-sentence communique shortly before markets opened on Tuesday, to the effect that the Federal Reserve stood ready to serve as a source of liquidity to support the economic and financial system. The Dow ended the day 5.9% higher, though most of the gains came after 1:00 p.m., and many blue chip stocks had failed to attract buyers during the early hours. Quibblers can talk all day about correlation, causation and coincidence, but people were scared out of their wits and were desperately hoping for a miracle. Alan Greenspan, who had stayed calm and collected throughout the storm, became a hero overnight.

Greenspan went on to cement his reputation as the most market-friendly Chairman in the history of the Federal Reserve. Traders could count on him to cut them some slack in the event of an adverse development, either through a flood of liquidity or lower interest rates. The term *Greenspan put* entered the economic lexicon, to describe the prevailing sentiment among traders. A *put option* is a derivative instrument that gives its buyer the right to sell a fixed number of shares at a predetermined price. Bullish investors buy put options as insurance against a sudden plunge in the price of the securities they own. With

Greenspan at the helm, everyone had an implicit put option, since he would never let the market fall beyond a point, or so the thinking went.

Yet not everyone viewed such levitations with levity. The Greenspan put was deemed by many economists as a *moral hazard*. The idea of privatizing gains and socializing losses has been mocked roundly throughout the modern era. An early example was the speech by President Andrew Jackson in 1834, castigating the representatives of the *Second Bank of the United States* who had come to persuade him to cough up funds for a bailout:

> *"I have had men watching you for a long time, and am convinced that you have used the funds of the bank to speculate in the breadstuffs of the country. When you won, you divided the profits amongst you, and when you lost, you charged it to the bank. You tell me that if I take the deposits from the bank and annul its charter, I shall ruin ten thousand families. That may be true, gentlemen, but that is your sin! Should I let you go on, you will ruin fifty thousand families, and that would be my sin! You are a den of vipers*

and thieves. I have determined to rout you out, and by the Eternal, I will rout you out!"

Presidents had real power back then.

Story 11: The Asian Financial Crisis

The slowdown in the Japanese economy in the early 1990s led to a rapid increase in foreign direct investment in various other South East Asian countries, including Indonesia, Malaysia, South Korea and Thailand. The GDPs of these countries grew at astonishingly high rates of 8%-12% through most of the 1990s. This created a positive feedback loop of higher GDP and higher FDI. All was well until the US dollar started strengthening around 1995-96, and soon there was a rapid flight of foreign investor capital. The central banks had a tough time defending the weakened currencies against the onslaught of speculators. The Thai currency *Baht* was the first to fall, and there was a domino effect that impacted almost all economies in South East Asia. Eventually, the IMF had to step in with $110 billion to stabilize the currencies, markets and economies.

From 1984 to 1997, the Baht was pegged to the US dollar at an exchange rate of 25. (1 US Dollar = 25 Baht.) During the early months of 1997, the flight of foreign investment led to bank failures and a credit crunch. *Finance One*, Thailand's largest investment bank and the epicentre of the crisis, collapsed after a merger with the *Thai Danu Bank,* announced in March, fell apart two months later. The government promised $3.9 billion to bailout banks and other distressed financial institutions in March, only to renege on the offer in June.

Defending the currency peg soon became an expensive exercise for the Bank of Thailand, and faced with rapidly dwindling foreign exchange reserves, the government finally decided to let the Baht float on 2 July 1997. By January 1998, the exchange rate had reached 56. The stock market fared even worse, with the benchmark SET index dropping more than 70% in two years – from 1410 in January 1996 to 360 in January 1998. Usually, an exporting nation will at least gain a competitive advantage when its currency depreciates. But by now, the financial crisis in Thailand had become a full-blown *Asian Financial Crisis*, and almost all currencies in South East Asia were getting hammered on a daily basis.

The situation was not without precedent. The *Mexican Peso Crisis* of 1994 had similar origins, triggered by a sudden devaluation of the peso by 15% in December 1994 by the newly elected President Ernesto Zedillo. The Mexican peso was pegged to the US dollar at the time, and the flight of capital eventually forced the government to let the currency float. In just a few weeks, inflation hit 52%, the contagion spread to the rest of Latin America, and the IMF had to intervene with a $50 billion bailout and all the austerity measures that come in tow.

One would imagine that the rest of the world would learn these lessons as if their life depended on it, and there would not be another crisis of comparable magnitude and consequences in less than three years. Yet every bubble comes with the tagline *"This time it's different"* emblazoned in gilded letters, and this time was no different. The roaring rally of the Asian tigers ended in tears.

Although the crisis began in Thailand, the effects were worse in Indonesia. The government abandoned the dollar peg of the currency *Rupiah* and let it float on 14 August 1997. The exchange rate fell by more than 12% in a single day, from 2663 to 2955, and bottomed out at 16800 in June 1998. The GDP contracted by 13.1% in 1998, and inflation peaked at 58%. Riots broke out throughout the country, leading to the resignation of President Suharto, who had been in power since 1966.

Malaysia, Singapore, South Korea and Hong Kong were also affected by the crisis. The second order effects of the crisis were a general feeling of risk-averseness and dampening of foreign investor sentiment in other emerging markets like Russia. This and other Russia-specific issues, like a huge fiscal deficit and rapid drop in crude oil prices, led to a series of speculative attacks on the *Rouble*. On 17 August 1998, the Russian government devalued the Rouble and announced a moratorium on the repayment of foreign debt. On 2 September, the dollar peg was abandoned and the Rouble was allowed to float. The exchange rate plunged from 6.29 on 17 August to 20.82 on 9 September.

The Russian default sent shockwaves down the global markets. The Dow Jones index fell nearly 20% in six weeks, from 9338 on 17 July to 7539 on 31 August. The resulting liquidity shock completely overwhelmed the *Long Term Capital Management* hedge fund, overseen by Robert Merton and Myron Scholes, pioneers of the Black-Scholes-Merton option pricing formula and winners of the 1997 Nobel Memorial Prize in Economics. On 23 September, the New York Fed President William McDonough convened an emergency meeting of representatives from fourteen banks, in an attempt to contain the fallout from a possible meltdown of the fund. In his book *When Genius Failed*, Roger Lowenstein describes the pressure cooker atmosphere at the meeting:

> *James Cayne, the cigar-chomping chief executive of Bear Stearns, had been vowing that he would stop clearing Long Term's trades – which would put it out of business – if the fund's available cash fell below $500 million. At the start of the year, that would have seemed remote, for Long Term's capital had been $4.7 billion. But during the past five weeks, or since Russia's*

default, Long Term had suffered numbing losses – day after day after day. Its capital was down to the minimum. Cayne didn't think it would survive another day.

The fund had already asked Warren Buffett for money. It had asked George Soros. It had gone to Merrill Lynch. One by one, it had asked every bank it could think of. Now it had no place left to go. That was why, like a godfather summoning rival and potentially warring families, McDonough had invited the banks. If each one moved to unload bonds individually, the result could be a worldwide panic. If they acted in concert, perhaps a catastrophe could be avoided. Although McDonough didn't say so, he wanted the banks to invest $4 billion and rescue the fund. He wanted them to do it right then – tomorrow would be too late.

McDonough's plan went through, and Alan Greenspan obliged with three quarter-point rate cuts in seven weeks, lowering the Fed funds rate to 4.75%. By November, the Dow was back above 9000. The Greenspan put was alive and well, and so was the global financial system.

Story 12: The Nasdaq Crash

Of the three rate cuts delivered in late 1998 by the Federal Reserve under Alan Greenspan, only the first one, announced on September 29, was widely expected. The second rate cut was delivered a mere 16 days after the first, on the day before the October options expiry and a month before the scheduled meeting of the Federal Open Market Committee (FOMC) where almost all rate decisions had been taken in the past. The markets rejoiced, and the Dow Jones index closed 4.1% higher.

Before the surprise October rate cut was announced, it was indeed expected that the FOMC would cut its rates at their next meeting, on November 17. The conventional wisdom, therefore, was that the interim rate cut in October was a case of front-loading the monetary easing. When the FOMC announced a *third* rate cut in seven weeks at the end of the meeting, the markets knew Greenspan had their back. By January, traders were partying like it was 1999 – because it was!

Monetary easing in the absence of a slowdown in growth always comes at a cost, and everyone at the Federal Reserve was aware that their actions could be setting up an asset bubble. It is possible that the turbulent and unexpected global events of the recent past persuaded the Fed that they should have enough safety margin to deal with the next unexpected development. As it turned out, the next unexpected development was their inappropriately wide safety margin itself.

The tech-heavy Nasdaq Composite index had closed above 1000 for the first time in 1995, had broken the 1500 barrier in 1997 and had gone past 2000 in July 1998. By January 1999, it had crossed 2500. Sensing that the elevated market valuations were fuelled by low interest rates, the Fed hiked the funds rate by a quarter-point in June, and again in August. But the markets kept going, primarily on the strength of internet-based companies (dotcoms) and an artificial boost in hardware and software sales in anticipation of the Y2K problem. On November 3, the Nasdaq Composite closed above 3000. Thirty days later, it zoomed past 3500, ignoring another quarter-point hike by the Fed. The share price of chipmaker Qualcomm Inc. had doubled from the start of the year by March, had doubled again by June, and *again* by October and **again** by December.

Surely this was a bubble? Surely it could only go down from here? Surely the sensible trade would be to short Nasdaq at 3500 and trust gravity to kick in at some point in the near future?

The way things turned out, the sensible trader would have gone bankrupt in the next few weeks. The Nasdaq Composite closed above 4000 on December 29, broke 4500 on February 17 and hit 5000 just three weeks later, on March 9. Meanwhile, the funds rate had reached 6%, thanks to two more hikes by the Fed, desperately trying to put the genie back in the bottle. The combined market capitalization of all the publicly listed US companies was 153% of the United States GDP, nearly twice the historical average. Then came the inevitable crash.

By October 2000, the Nasdaq Composite had fallen below 3000, a level not to be seen again until March 2012. By January 2001, it had gone under 2500, and even that level was revisited only in 2007. The index bottomed out at 1108 in October 2002. Qualcomm shares fell more than 85% from the lofty heights scaled in 1999. California had not seen such an earthquake since 1906.

Story 13: Lehman Brothers

The Federal Reserve was quick to bring interest rates down again in the aftermath of the Nasdaq crash. Over a period of 18 months, the funds rate was brought down from 6.5% in May 2000 all the way to 2% in November 2001. The 9/11 terrorist attack was an additional source of economic disruption, at least in the short term. The Fed funds rate hit 1% in June 2003 for the first time in more than 40 years, and stayed there till June 2004. Plenty of time to create asset bubbles, and that is exactly what happened. For a change, this time the bubble was in real estate, not equities.

Between 2001 and 2005, there was a widespread housing boom in the United States. The down payments required for home ownership were at all-time lows. Moreover, financial instruments known as *mortgage-backed securities* allowed home loans to be neatly packaged into tranches and sold in the secondary market as *collateralized debt obligations* to counterparties who took on the risk of default in exchange for high yield. Such innovations widened the ambit of home ownership even to people with subprime credit, while the small down payments and very low interest rates increased affordability and resulted in inflated home prices. These home prices, in turn, served as collateral for extravagant lifestyle and speculative financial transactions, like buying a second home for the sole purpose of selling it at a profit – with no intention of ownership.

In August 2005, University of Chicago economist Raghuram Rajan, who would later head the Reserve Bank of India between 2013 and 2016, gave a speech at the annual Jackson Hole Economic Symposium. The main theme of his speech was whether financial innovations and deregulation during the Greenspan era had made the world riskier. To quote an excerpt:

> Banks now require more liquid markets to hedge some of the risks associated with the complicated products they have created or guarantees they have offered. Their greater reliance on market liquidity can make their

balance sheets more suspect in times of crisis, making them less able to provide the liquidity assurance that they have provided in the past. Clearly, some of the more sophisticated banks fully understand this. Whether they have adjusted fully for that great unknown, the behavior of other market participants, is unclear.

Taken together, these trends suggest that even though there are far more participants who are able to absorb risk today, the financial risks that are being created by the system are indeed greater. And even though there should theoretically be a diversity of opinion and actions by market participants, and a greater capacity to absorb risk, competition and compensation may induce more correlation in behavior than is desirable. While it is hard to be categorical about anything as complex as the modern financial system, it is possible that these developments are creating more financial-sector induced procyclicality than in the past. They may also create a greater (albeit still small) probability of a catastrophic meltdown.

These cautious remarks were dismissed as founded on "Luddite premises" by former Treasury Secretary Lawrence Summers. But the words turned out to be as prescient as they were prudent. By early 2007, it became quite clear that all was not well, and it certainly was not going to end well.

The canary in the coal mine was *Bear Stearns*, an investment bank neck-deep in exposure to subprime mortgages. Moreover, the position was highly leveraged – each dollar of the firm's capital supported more than $35 in assets. By March 2008, it was clear that Bear Stearns would not survive much longer, and after the markets closed for the week on 14 March, the Federal Reserve mediated a stock swap sale of the company to the rival banking firm JP Morgan Chase. The Bear Stearns stock had traded at $68 on March 12 and had closed above $30 on 14 March, yet the offered price was a paltry $2 per share. (The final acquisition price was sweetened to $10 per share a week later, after a shareholder revolt threatened to derail the deal.) Life had come full circle for CEO James Cayne, who nearly brought the world to its knees by demanding his pound of flesh during the 1998 LTCM crisis, and nearly brought the world to its knees again in 2008 by blowing up so spectacularly. The Federal Reserve also announced a hefty rate cut at its scheduled meeting on 18 March, lowering the funds rate from 3% to 2.25%.

The toll from the subprime mortgage crisis continued to rise in the subsequent months. There were ten bank failures in the United States between January 2008 and August 2008, same as the number of bank failures in the previous *five years*. All hell broke loose in September, when the government sponsored enterprises *Fannie Mae* (Federal National Mortgage Association) and *Freddie Mac* (Federal Home Loan Mortgage Association) were placed under the conservatorship of the Federal Housing Finance Agency. These "credit events" triggered financial instruments known as *credit default swaps* and resulted in huge losses to many institutions who had sold them for what had appeared to be relatively risk-free income. The insurance giant *American International Group* (AIG) had to be bailed out by the US Treasury for $182 billion with taxpayer money, although in this case the taxpayers ended up making a healthy profit of $23 billion when the Treasury sold the last of its acquired shares in 2012.

The only major institution that could not be saved was *Lehman Brothers*, the fourth largest investment bank in the world, as it was facing a *solvency crisis*, as opposed to the *liquidity crisis* of Bear Stearns and AIG. Treasury Secretary Henry Paulson, in his memoir *On the Brink* describes the predicament of government officials and investment bank CEOs trying to work out a deal to prevent an imminent bankruptcy of Lehman Brothers:

"We're working hard on a transaction, and we need to know where you guys stand," I said. "If there's a capital hole, the government can't fill it. So how do we get this done?"

I can only imagine what was going through their minds. These were smart, tough businessmen and they were in a difficult spot. We were asking them to rescue one competitor by helping to finance its sale to yet another competitor. But they had no idea about the state of Lehman's books, or how much they would have to cough up to support such a deal. Without this information, they were flying blind: they could not predict the consequences of any course of action they chose. They knew how important it was to maintain a smoothly functioning market and how much we needed them to keep lending to one another if Lehman did go down. But their own institutions were all under grave pressure, and they had no idea what tests they might face in the days ahead – or whether they would be strong enough to survive this crisis.

In the end, there was no deal. On September 15, Lehman Brothers filed for bankruptcy protection before the markets opened, declaring $639 billion in assets and $619 billion in debt. The Dow Jones index fell 4.4% that day, marking the beginning of a downturn that would eventually see a drop of 54% from the October 2007 highs before bottoming out in March 2009. The shockwaves would lead to the destruction of trillions of dollars of wealth in the United States and the rest of the world. The Volatility Index (VIX) of the Chicago Board Options Exchange, nicknamed the *fear gauge* of US markets, hit monthly highs of 89.53, 81.48 and 68.61 in the last three months of 2008. Barring these three months, the index has never traded above 51 since its inception in 1993 to the present day.

In a Congressional hearing held a few weeks after the bankruptcy of Lehman Brothers, as the carnage lay in plain sight, many lawmakers wanted to know why the Federal Reserve and the US Treasury did not step in to rescue Lehman Brothers. The simple answer, as explained by both Henry Paulson and Fed Chair Ben Bernanke (who had succeeded Greenspan in 2006), was that neither the Treasury nor the Federal Reserve had the constitutional authority to use taxpayer money for that purpose. The Congress soon passed legislation to remove this handicap, and launched the Troubled Asset Relief Program (TARP) – a $700 billion rescue package that ensured there would not be another Lehman event. On 25 November, the Federal Reserve, running out of room to cut interest rates, officially launched quantitative easing, announcing the purchase of mortgage-backed securities and government bonds, injecting much-needed liquidity into the markets. On 16 December, the Fed lowered the funds target to the 0%-0.25% range, where they would remain for seven years.

Story 14: Quantitative Easing

As we have seen, quantitative easing (QE) was pioneered by the Bank of Japan in 2001 as a response to several years of stagnant growth and persistent deflation. When the Federal Reserve launched similar measures in November 2008, many economists thought that it was only intended as a stopgap measure with a limited shelf life, in view of the huge fiscal deficit it would entail and the runaway inflation it could potentially provoke. The fiscal deficit did balloon to astronomical levels, but the Congress realized that QE was the best of the available alternatives and ignored the mounting deficit in largely bipartisan fashion. As for inflation, it remained rather tame – staying below 3% all the way until April 2011.

By the beginning of 2009, the liquidity collapse in the aftermath of the Lehman bankruptcy had resulted in full-blown recessions all over the world. While the Bank of England and the Bank of Japan also took the QE route to fight the crisis, the European Central Bank (ECB) President Jean-Claude Trichet was initially reluctant to follow suit. By May 2009, with the economies of Portugal, Italy, Greece and Spain (lumped under the rather undignified acronym *PIGS*) reeling under a sovereign debt crisis that posed an existential threat to the Eurozone, the ECB was convinced that there was no real alternative and promptly launched QE.

Why is quantitative easing such a big deal? After all, don't central banks buy government debt all the time as part of open market operations? Well, they do, but purchases under open market operations stop as soon as the target interest rate is attained, whereas quantitative easing ensures that the central bank will continue to buy bonds indefinitely. There is a difference between Jack and Jill turning the tap on to fill a pail of water, and Jack and Jill keeping the tap on till the water tank runs dry. Quantitative easing is the only antidote to a catastrophic liquidity crunch, such as the one that credit markets encountered after the collapse of Lehman Brothers.

The flipside of quantitative easing was the

extremely low yield on bonds, and by extension, on deposit rates. This put an unfair burden on retirees and senior citizens, who were accustomed to meeting their living expenses by means of interest accrued on their lifetime savings. Pension fund managers were also forced to chase more risk than would be prudent, as there was hardly any return in the fixed income space. The high-flying bankers of Wall Street had made the world of finance an unnecessarily risky place – not just for themselves, but for everyone else as well.

While Trichet was rather circumspect about QE, his successor Mario Draghi, who began his eight-year term in November 2011, had no qualms about asset purchases. In 2012, at a global investment conference in London, he demonstrated his resolve to defend the *Euro*, and by extension the heterogeneous economies comprising the Eurozone, using any and all means necessary:

Within our mandate, the ECB is ready to do whatever it takes to preserve the euro. And believe me, it will be enough.

There are some short-term challenges, to say the least. The short-term challenges in our view relate mostly to the financial fragmentation that has taken place in the euro area. Investors retreated within their national boundaries. The interbank market is not functioning. It is only functioning very little within each country by the way, but it is certainly not functioning across countries.

And I think the key strategy point here is that if we want to get out of this crisis, we have to repair this financial fragmentation.

The fragmentation challenge was addressed by the introduction of the *Single Supervisory Mechanism* (SSM) in 2014, under which all the important credit institutions in the Eurozone were placed under the direct supervision of the ECB. Indeed, the ECB had, and continues to have, the unique challenge of dealing with conflicts of national sovereignty while implementing decisions uniformly across member nations – a challenge not faced by any other central bank in the world. The ECB also introduced several unconventional measures including negative deposit rates, Targeted Long

Term Refinancing Operations (TLTROs) and Outright Monetary Transactions (OMTs), all intended to aid the transmission of monetary policy and stimulate greater lending by banks.

Negative deposit rates might sound like a quaint idea, but in practice it is already encountered in any economy where the interest on deposits is lower than the rate of inflation. The whole rationale of banks giving interest on the funds of depositors is based on our commonsense notion that a dollar today is worth more than a dollar next year. In a deflationary setting, this is no longer the case, and the banks are justified in charging a 'parking fee', much as they would for a safe deposit locker. TLTROs were essentially subsidy programmes offered by the ECB to institutions who could not afford to lend at the prevailing very low rates. Finally, OMTs were announced to indicate willingness on the part of the ECB to buy distressed sovereign debt under specific conditions. It was not used even once – the announcement itself turned out to be sufficient to calm the markets and keep the bond yields stable. It was a great illustration of

Theodore Roosevelt's old maxim: *"Speak softly and carry a big stick; you will go far."*

Chapter 4: The Impossible Trinity

In the 1960s, economists Robert Mundell and John Fleming, independently of each other, showed that a central bank cannot attain three seemingly desirable goals at the same time. This came to be known in academic circles as the *Mundell-Fleming trilemma*, but soon received a more glamorous appellation, namely *The Impossible Trinity*. The three goals in question are **an independent monetary policy, a fixed foreign exchange rate and free movement of capital**. Stated differently, any central bank that wishes to have an independent monetary policy and a fixed exchange rate for its currency (e.g. a peg to the US dollar) must institute capital controls, i.e., restrictions on foreign exchange transactions by its citizens and businesses.

The argument was quite simple. If two nations pursue monetary policies independently of each other, optimizing the well-being of their own economies, there is no reason to believe that a fixed exchange rate between their currencies would hold indefinitely. If there are no capital controls, the artificially maintained exchange rate that no longer reflects the relative prices of goods and services in the two countries will offer an opportunity for arbitrage. The central bank will wage a losing battle to defend the peg with all its foreign currency reserves, and sooner or later, will run out of said reserves. Truth will prevail over propaganda.

This was a highly insightful observation, and as often happens to an idea whose time is ripe, was discovered almost simultaneously by more than one person. Yet it remained within the confines of academia and did not have much of a policy impact. The reason was that capital controls were practically the norm in the Bretton Woods era, and with the exception of a few economists like Robert Triffin, hardly anyone thought that its collapse was only a few years away. Even after 1971, the free movement of capital did not happen overnight, and it took many years of persuasion before developing nations agreed to the experiment.

It was only in the 1990s, with the *Mexican Peso Crisis* of 1994, the *Asian Financial Crisis* of

1997 and the *Russian Default* of 1998, that governments and policymakers started taking the Impossible Trinity seriously. It was the same story on all three occasions. The Mexican Peso, the Thai Baht, the Indonesian Rupiah and the Russian Rouble were all pegged to the dollar, and were all considerably weakened by a sudden shift in the monetary policy of the United States and the consequent strengthening of the US dollar. In all cases, the respective central banks were down to spare change on their foreign currency reserves before they conceded defeat and allowed the currency to float. Abandoning a long-standing peg at the precise moment when a currency is at its weakest and asking it to fend for itself is a recipe for disaster, and we have seen in the previous pages the disasters that ensued in all these countries. It is also worthwhile to note that countries like India and China, who had not abandoned capital controls at the time, emerged relatively unscathed from the Asian Financial Crisis.

Developed economies have also courted peril by ignoring the Impossible Trinity. A classic example is the withdrawal of the pound sterling from the *European Exchange Rate Mechanism* (EERM) after the Bank of England failed to defend the exchange rate of *1 British Pound = 2.78 Deutsche Mark*. The *Quantum Fund* of legendary investor George Soros had built up a substantial short position of $1.5 billion against the British pound, which was dramatically increased to $10 billion on 16 September 1992. In response, the Bank of England started buying pounds in the open market to defend the peg, announced an emergency increase in the benchmark interest rate from 10% to 12% and declared the willingness to raise it to 15% if necessary. But the selling continued unabated, as the economic fundamentals did not justify the exchange rate implied by the currency peg. By the end of the day, the authorities had no choice but to leave the EERM and let the pound float. It was a rare instance of a hedge fund calling the bluff of a central bank and actually winning. The day was dubbed by the British press as *Black Wednesday*, but Soros made the princely profit of one billion dollars in a single day. After all, short-term currency trading is a zero-sum game.

Chapter 5: Inflation Targeting

In the early chapters of this book, we saw that the main objectives of monetary policy were stable prices, maximum employment and balanced economic growth, in that order. However, the instruments available at the disposal of central banks, such as open market operations, the discount rate and reserve requirements were all geared towards the primary mandate of stable prices, although they did have secondary effects that eventually led to the achievement of the other two goals. In 1952, Dutch economist Jan Tinbergen, who would go on to share the inaugural Nobel Memorial Prize in Economics with Ragnar Frisch in 1969, published a highly influential treatise titled *On The Theory of Economic Policy* in which he argued that governments should use as many instruments as the number of objectives of their economic policy, no more and no less. Too few instruments can result in situations where some of the objectives will have to be sacrificed, whereas too many instruments will lead to multiple solutions and redundancy. The basic idea is the same as the well-known result in elementary linear algebra that a linearly independent system of m equations in n variables has a unique solution if and only if m=n. This preference for the equality of objectives and instruments came to be known as the *Tinbergen Rule*.

It must be noted that the Tinbergen rule is a holistic statement about economic policy as a whole, without any compartmentalization such as fiscal or monetary policy. It might well be the case that fiscal policy can address unemployment more effectively, while monetary policy can address inflation more effectively. It would still make sense to conduct fiscal policy in a manner that does not aggravate inflation, and to conduct monetary policy in a manner that does not aggravate unemployment. Moreover, one can always work with a single objective function expressed as a linear combination (i.e., a priority-weighted sum) of the elementary objectives.

In 1989, the New Zealand government, frustrated with unsuccessful attempts to bring inflation under control, amended the Reserve

Bank Act to set price stability as the *only* goal of monetary policy, with the understanding that fiscal policy would take care of everything else. The new Act came into force in February 1990, and the Reserve Bank Governor Donald Brash was given the responsibility to keep inflation below 3% during his tenure. He did such a fine job that he kept getting reappointed, seeing six different Prime Ministers in office during his fourteen years as Governor. Meanwhile, other nations took note of the effectiveness of the new policy, which came to be called *inflation targeting*. Canada switched to inflation targeting in 1991, and the United Kingdom in 1992. As of 2019, more than thirty central banks have adopted inflation targeting, including Australia (1993), Brazil (1999), USA (2012), Japan (2013) and India (2016).

Since the management of expectations of inflation is a crucial aspect of managing inflation, central banks do not merely set inflation targets – they make public announcements of their targets from time to time, along with potential upside and downside risks to the targets. A clear advantage of inflation targeting is a reduction in interference from politicians and bureaucrats, as the demarcation of responsibilities result in far fewer turf wars. Inflation targeting also brings greater accountability of central banks in a democratic framework and shields them from a lot of criticism that would otherwise occur in their struggle to attain incompatible goals. The only real downsides are the loss of flexibility and discretion, as well as the opportunity cost of not being able to do more in times of economic distress, for fear of overstepping the policy mandate.

Chapter 6: The Taylor Rule

The great challenge of macroeconomics is to come up with models that explain the evolution of, and the relationship between, aggregate economic indicators like inflation, unemployment and GDP. The impact of fiscal and monetary policies on these indicators are worthy of quantitative analysis in their own right, as governments and central banks are actively interested in controlling them to maximize the collective welfare of the population. In 1993, Stanford economist John Taylor published a research paper titled *Discretion Versus Policy Rules in Practice* in which he introduced a model of monetary policy that closely approximated actual policy actions of the Federal Reserve during the previous six years. At the heart of the model was a deceptively simple equation in the form of a feedback rule, which came to be known as the *Taylor Rule*.

The Taylor Rule refers to the equation $r=1.5p+0.5y+1$ where r is the Fed funds rate, p is the rate of inflation averaged over the previous four quarters, and y is the percentage deviation of (real) GDP from the GDP implied by the long-term economic growth rate based on the previous ten years of data. (The long-term growth rate was taken as 2.2% in Taylor's paper.) Taylor showed how the Fed funds rate as predicted by the rule was close to the actual Fed funds rate from 1987 to 1992, a period marked by turbulent and unexpected events like the Gulf War and German unification. As a first approximation, the 3:1 ratio between the coefficients corresponding to inflation and growth was indicative of their relative weightage in the policy decisions of the Federal Reserve.

While it is not all that difficult to come up with a *post hoc* model of central bank behaviour, the Taylor rule continued to be predictive of the Federal Reserve's monetary policy decisions well into the new millennium. It was only around 2003, with Alan Greenspan lowering rates all the way to 1% in a desperate attempt to prop up the stock market following the Nasdaq crash, that monetary policy started deviating significantly from the path predicted by the Taylor Rule. Most economists now agree that it was the Federal Reserve that was in error, not the Taylor Rule. However, in the aftermath of the Lehman Brothers bankruptcy and the advent of quantitative easing, it is generally agreed that the Taylor Rule and its analogues in other economies, although still valid in spirit, might require a fresh examination of the coefficients as well as additional variables. Boris Hofmann and Bilyana Bogdanova, researchers at the *Bank for International Settlements* (BIS), an international financial institution that functions as a central bank for central banks, conclude their paper *Taylor Rules and Monetary Policy: A Great Global Deviation?* with a reminder of the limitations of relying exclusively on the Taylor Rule in analysing monetary policy:

> *First, the indications of Taylor rules should be taken with caution as they involve assumptions about unobservable concepts which might be wrong and hence misleading. Specifically, the indication that monetary policy has been systematically too accommodative might in part reflect a drop in equilibrium real interest rates. Second, the traditional Taylor rule might not adequately capture the factors that are relevant for macroeconomic stability and hence for monetary policy. In particular, financial stability risks and their macroeconomic*

implications are not appropriately captured. As a consequence, the Taylor rule is likely to have a downward bias during financial booms and an upward bias during financial busts. Finally, Taylor rules do not capture the role of other monetary policy instruments. Specifically, changes in reserve requirements, which play an important role in some EMEs, and central banks' balance sheet policies are not taken into account. Total assets held by central banks have roughly quadrupled over the past decade and stood at approximately $18 trillion at the beginning of 2012, or roughly 30% of global GDP. This is likely to have further eased monetary policy, e.g. by lowering long-term interest rates and mitigating exchange rate appreciation, so that the global monetary policy stance over the sample period was probably more accommodative than indicated by the level of policy rates.

In spite of such drawbacks, there is no doubt that the Taylor Rule has been a valuable addition to the principles of central banking. One cannot expect the laws of economics to be as precise as the laws of physics, and even rudimentary steps towards a calculus of human behaviour must be viewed with charity and gratitude. As we have seen, central banking has come a long way in the past hundred years, and the next hundred years may offer challenges that are unlike anything encountered in the past. For example, in an era of widespread automation and universal basic income, how would the dynamics of inflation change, what would drive economic growth, and what would unemployment even *mean?* We can only speculate about the evolution of monetary policy in times drastically different from our own, but if history is any guide, the backdrop of liberal democratic institutions, unencumbered markets and a culture of innovation will help us tide over any teething troubles that may arise in our transition to the next stage of civilization.

www.ingramcontent.com/pod-product-compliance
Lightning Source LLC
Chambersburg PA
CBHW070658220526
45466CB00001B/490